THIS IS
NOT THE
FINAL
CHAPTER

THIS IS
NOT THE
FINAL
CHAPTER

A Memoir of Faith, Strength and Tenacity

ROBIN R. HAYNES

Printed in the United States of America

ISBN: 978-1-64484-187-7

Special discounts are available on bulk quantity purchases by book clubs, associations and special interest groups. For details email: sales@publishyourgift.com or call (888) 949-6228.
For information log on to www.PublishYourGift.com

This project is dedicated to individuals who feel as if their current situation is the final chapter. I want to inform you that you have new chapters to create.

TABLE OF CONTENTS

ACKNOWLEDGMENTS

First, I give honor to GOD who continues to sustain me. All I can say is, GOD, You are amazing.

To my son, Ryan, you truly are my reason why. I love you. I am extremely proud of the young man that you have become. Thank you for believing in me through the good and not-so-good times. With the assistance from GOD, we overcame the challenges that were presented to us.

To my parents, Robert Sr. and Patricia, your prayers, love, and continued support are priceless. Words are simply not enough to express my gratitude.

To my siblings, Robert Jr. and Hope, where do I begin? Thank you for simply being in my corner at all times. Thank you for loving me unconditionally and for giving me the gifts of my precious nieces: Eden, Jordan, and Madison.

To my grandmother, Mrs. Annie Mae Williams, thank you for providing a solid foundation for us. To my grandmother, Mrs. Bertie Rhodes-Gibson, although you are no longer with us physically, your spirit and memory still dwell in your children, grandchildren, and great-grandchildren. I miss you so much!

To my family both near and far, thank you for your continued prayers and support.

Aisha and the Aisha Photography team, thank you for always making me beautiful. Dominick, Mark, and the entire Different Regard team, thank you for being the world's best stylists and designers. Tieshena and the Purposely Created Publishing Group team, thank you for accepting this project and allowing me to share my story on your platform.

Cristel, who would have thought almost three years ago you'd become one of my dearest friends? I appreciate you more than you know. Pat, thank you for your ear and for allowing me to bounce this project off of you. Carmen, Jerry, Keisha, and Aisha, twenty years later, we're still rocking, and I am honored to have you all in my life.

Finally, to my readers, followers, students, clients, and audiences, THANK YOU for taking this journey with me and for allowing me to share my story with you all.

FOREWORD

In retrospect, Robin R. Haynes—my eldest and only sister—was likely one of my first close encounters with the strength and resilience of a woman of color. After all, like most brown girls in America, we come from a lineage of women who have overcome seemingly insurmountable obstacles to achieve great feats, giving birth to change agents. The template for a change agent is often one who ventures off the beaten path; one who bends, shatters, or blatantly ignores the rules; one whose dreams seem unrealistic. Venturing off the path immediately places you in the realm of uncertainty. Onlookers are often skeptical, judgmental, and pessimistic about the end result. The strong—like Robin—use these things as fuel for perseverance.

From birth, Robin has blazed her own trail. She gave birth to her only child at the age of twenty. While her friends continued their educational pursuits and her youngest sister ventured off to college, she was honing her life skills. During early adulthood, Robin started her career in the financial industry where she steadily climbed the corporate ladder with a high school diploma and a few college credits. During that time, she returned to school and obtained her bachelor's degree in accounting.

Despite her early success in the financial industry, she decided to take her thirteen years of experience and venture into entrepreneurship, establishing Understanding Finances. The company provided financial management and basic, sound financial advice for everyday people, promoting saving through basic budgeting, distinguishing between needs and wants, and reviewing the various traditional banking options. These topics formed the foundation for her first published project, *The Fundamentals of Finances Applied to Everyday Living*.

Anyone who spends even a moment with Robin—who is fully committed to empowering the community—can hear her asking, "Are you understanding your finances?"

Robin's self-taught strategies for saving would prove beneficial when her household built on two incomes was forced to survive on her solo entrepreneur's salary. She put her skills into overdrive, pulling herself up by her bootstraps, ultimately securing *two* full-time jobs, getting her son off to college, obtaining her master's degree in entrepreneurship, and writing this great work. She has become a beacon of light for entrepreneurship, small business ownership, and financial sustainability throughout the world. If you are looking for inspiration, if you need a story of triumph, and if you need ways to overcome financial challenges, allow Robin's story to encourage and enlighten you. She has and continues to inspire me along my journey.

Hope Elizabeth Rhodes-Pretlow,
MD, MPH, FAAP

"And let us not be weary in well doing: for in due season we shall reap, if we faint not."
—Galatians 6:9

INTRODUCTION

On June 29, 2019, GOD spoke to my spirit and instructed me to share my story. Waking up baffled, I asked GOD why. He simply said, "Trust me." With that said, I ran into my office and started sketching out the specifics for this project.

Unlike the first project, *The Fundamentals of Finances Applied to Everyday Living*, where I discuss various financial strategies, this project is personal. It shares how I was able to persevere and overcome very challenging times.

Although at times life can be challenging, believe it or not, we have the ability to control the outcome of those challenges. The purpose of this story is to encourage, enlighten, inspire, and inform you that you have the capability to overcome various trials that arise in your life.

THE BEGINNING

"Life is what happens to us while we are
making other plans."
—Allen Saunders, Journalist

Life can be challenging, as we all know. It's up to us, however, to control the climate of those challenging times. What does this mean? In simplistic terms, it means that we have the ability to change the narrative within our situation. If you don't think you have it in you, I strongly encourage you to listen and really soak in my journey from 2012 to now, and you'll understand that you have the capability, just as I did.

It's funny how life works. As a financial coach, never in a million years did I think I'd be in some of the most difficult—and I do mean difficult—financial situations. Because I'm a financial coach, you would think that I'd have it together at all times. I'm here to tell you that when life hits, *life hits*. However, through life's experiences, I've learned that difficult times won't last.

My mental transition into the next phase of my life began in 2012 when I received my undergraduate degree in accounting. I received a phone call from my aunt who, at the time, worked for the college that I was about to graduate from. During the conversation, she said, "Congratulations, your name is in the graduation program. It's official." Talk about excited. You see, both my sister and brother had earned their undergraduate and graduate degrees, and me—well, I had all this banking experience but no degree, so furthering my education at this later point in my life was a huge milestone for me.

Before graduating, GOD spoke to my spirit and instructed me to teach his people about the importance of understanding their financial picture. Having thirteen years of banking experience at this point, I had no idea that GOD had given and trusted me with the gift of finances. With the gift that I've been blessed with came *a lot* of valleys. Looking back, I am appreciative of those valleys because they've shaped me into the woman who I've become.

And so my story begins.

I THOUGHT I KNEW

"Life is trying things to see if they work."
—Ray Bradbury, Author

June 2012

I had officially graduated with my undergraduate degree. Soon after I graduated, I launched my first business, Understanding Finances. After registering my business with the state of Maryland, I hired someone to create my logo and website. You see, being a business owner was all new to me. I thought I knew what I was doing, but looking back, I was an uneducated new business owner. I had no business coach to hold my hand, therefore, I went against all of the business fundamentals that I now know and currently teach my audiences and clients.

Once I registered my business, I became arrogant. I went into work (yes, I was still fully employed at the time) and shared with my colleagues that I had registered my business. I showed them my newly designed logo, which, looking back, was a mess. Needless to say, at that point, I was overconfident simply because I had my undergraduate degree in accounting, my business was registered, my logo was designed, and my business cards were on the way.

One day, after having worked my eight-hour shift, I got called into my manager's office. During our meeting, I received a corrective action, the basis of which being that I had given a client a hard time. Keep in mind that I was known as a good employee. I was never called out for non-performance, and I always went above and beyond my assigned duties. Receiving a corrective action was something that I couldn't wrap my head around, and I knew it was time for me to leave. Sometimes, when you don't move when GOD says to, GOD will allow things to happen so that you have no choice but to move.

I started constructing my exit plan. I looked at all the time that I had accrued off from 1999 to 2012, which included personal, sick, and vacation days, to see how I could deplete all of my sick and personal leave. For the first phase of my plan, I called my primary care physician and requested documentation that covered me to be out for two weeks. I had a total of eighty-eight hours of sick leave, which was two weeks and one day, and I used all but eight hours.

The second phase of my plan involved using all of my personal time because, if you leave a company, your personal leave cannot be paid out. After I returned from my two-week "illness" on a Tuesday, I went on my annual family vacation to Virginia Beach that Thursday. Once I returned from my vacation, I had my manager transition my vacation time to personal time. About two weeks after using all of my leave, I walked into my management team's office and turned in my resignation. Although this was hard for me, I knew that my time with the organization had come to an end.

Wow. Did I tell my job that I was leaving without another job lined up? I did. I know—insane! *Before I continue, I would suggest that unless you have money saved to sustain you, don't follow my actions. Trust me.*

After I submitted my resignation letter, I started cleaning out my desk. I couldn't believe I had been at this organization for thirteen years. I had started off in 1999 as a teller and worked my way up to a financial services consultant. Being in the financial industry was something that was dear to me, as I had been doing it for a long time.

As my time with this organization was coming to an end, I was between emotions. On one side, I was a bit sad due to the relationships that I had formed; on the other side, I was excited because I was on the cusp of starting a new chapter in my life. My time at the organization taught me everything I knew up to this particular point about the financial industry, from counting cash straps to balancing vaults to processing loans, which included how to read and understand a credit report and how to calculate a debt to income. Yes, I had learned a lot! Not only had I gained my financial education here, but some of my best friendships were birthed at this job. And it was coming to an end. Again, I was sad, but I also knew that GOD had other plans for me.

The last day at this organization that I practically grew up in finally came. As I walked out of the building, carrying my box of stuff from my office, I looked at the building and started crying. A huge part of my adult life was coming to an end, and I was about to embark on another chapter of my life. I was scared and nervous all at once.

Soon after leaving my employer, I fully launched the Understanding Finances consulting business. While the launch of my business was still new, I used my retirement account for income and for paying my half of the household expenses (another hard lesson that I would learn).

Fall 2012

While attending a business event, I met an individual who worked for one of the largest radio stations in

Baltimore. As this young lady and I chatted, I shared my line of work.

"Have you ever considered a radio show?" she asked.

With a puzzled look, I said, "No, I haven't considered a radio broadcast."

"Well, you have a message that people need to hear," the young lady continued, "and you need your own radio show."

The young lady wanted me to educate listeners on their finances. As she and I continued to talk, it dawned on me that it would be awesome if I had my own radio show. After all, what did I have to lose? The young lady and I closed the conversation with setting up a time and date to finalize the radio broadcast contract for October 2012. I was about to have my own radio show!

At this same event, I met the publishing team who published my first book, *The Fundamentals of Finances Applied to Everyday Living*. What captured my attention about this team was the book cover of one of the cofounders of the publishing group. I loved seeing successful African Americans. Both members of the team had written several projects, including books, screenplays, and short films.

As we all started talking, the publishing team asked, "Have you considered writing a book?"

I again said, "No." I had no idea of how to even write a book, let alone discuss the many logistics that went along with launching a written project.

As we wrapped up the conversation, the publishing team said, "You should consider writing a book."

I knew that GOD had allowed me to encounter these individuals at this event for a reason. A few weeks after the event, I contacted the publishing team and agreed to write the book. It was November 2012 when I signed my first publishing contract. Wow—I was now a radio host and was about to write my first book. Talk about being scared and excited at the same time. It appeared that everything was lining up.

2013

While hosting my radio show and writing my manuscript, I was also facilitating various components for my business, which included lecturing and coaching clients on strengthening their financial picture. After I submitted the first draft of the book, the publishing team's response was not exactly positive. They said, "Robin, you're doing a lot of things, but are you making any money? This isn't what we are looking for in terms of content. Robin, tell the financial story. You know finances."

I had written some content about finances, which included terminology, however, they were looking for more of a story. After having this conversation, I was insulted. After all, I had been in the financial industry going on thirteen years. This was definitely a coachable moment. I took an assessment of everything that I was doing and realized that I was hardly making any money. I was doing everything I could, and *I wasn't making any money*. This was because I had no business plan, nor did I know who my target clients were. I launched my business without a plan. Talk about a wake-up call. I honestly hadn't really thought about the financial component of the business. The irony of this was that I was a financial coach. I knew about personal finances, but I knew nothing about running a business. Again, I had no business coach to guide me or hold my hand. As I was still trying to figure out how to make money from my business, I was still using my retirement account to supplement my income.

Following the extremely hard teaching moment, I finally got the modified manuscript approved. I was relieved and excited that the publishing team had given me the green light to proceed. Next, we worked on the cover, the sizing, and the rest of the logistics for the final product. That meant more lessons that I was being taught—and more money that was being spent but not being replaced. Finally, the day came when the final product was released. In March 2013, I became a published author! To this day, it still amazes me that I am a published author.

I thought 2013 was going to be my year. The book was launched, I still had my radio show where I talked about the importance of financial sustainability, and my coaching clients were starting to increase. I had the mindset that when the book was released, I was going to make an abundance of money. But things did not go as I had envisioned. After the book signing, book sales were extremely slow. The radio show was financially bleeding me dry, as I was continuously paying to host a live broadcast. Eventually, I had to discontinue the show. Financially, things were starting to spiral out of control.

LIFE HAPPENS

2014

Having been in the financial industry as long as I have and knowing the importance of maintaining a healthy financial picture, never did I imagine that I personally would experience financial challenges.

After the decline in sales of my first book, and the discontinuation of the radio show, my savings account was dwindling fast. With everything I had going on, due to no fault of anyone's, my marriage was on the cusp of ending. Having a kid and getting married at an early age—well, let's just say we grow up, we mature, and we change from the people we once were. *It's okay.*

My ex-husband and I officially separated in July 2014. My son and I were alone in a house that was created with two full-time incomes. At this point, we barely had half of an income. I thought my life was pretty much over. All the while, on the outside, I pretended everything was okay. Let's be honest—we have a tendency to mask our emotions and feelings, pretending things are okay when they really aren't. I felt like a failure, even as a published author. I had failed my son, and more importantly, I had failed myself.

By December of that year, while everyone was in the holiday spirit, I was trying to find ways I could keep myself financially afloat. At this point, my savings were down to nothing, and my retirement account—which I had been using to pay all of the household expenses—had dwindled. As I began to close the year, I thought to myself that 2015 had to be better than this. At that point, I had no idea why GOD was punishing me. Looking back, HE wasn't punishing me; HE was preparing me.

2015

When January came around, I was ready for a new year, a new outlook. At this point, I was two years out of corporate America, so now was not the time to be particular while looking for employment. Having done all I could do in terms of running my business, which was not financially successful, I realized that I needed to have a steady stream of income. The reality was, I had bills to pay and two mouths to feed, so I decided to return to work as an employee. I applied for employment, only to be told "I'm underqualified" or "I'm overqualified." Why couldn't I just be qualified?

While applying for various job opportunities, I came across a life insurance agent position. One of the requirements of the position was to have a life insurance license, which I had. Soon after I applied for the position, I received a call for an interview. A few days later, I was hired. During the interview process, the interviewer, who was also the hiring manager, made the compensation package look very attractive. I was extremely excited to finally get back in the position where I didn't have to worry about how I was going to pay my bills.

But not so fast. When I received my first paycheck, I felt deflated again! After being in the field educating indviduals on the importance of life insurance, I recieved a very small paycheck. I thought to myself, *how am I going to pay my bills with this?* I thought I had understood how the compensation worked as a commissioned employee, but clearly I didn't. I was used to receiving a normal paycheck every two weeks. Once the initial shock wore off, I convinced myself that my future paychecks would get better once I finalized more policies.

Then, I did something that I promised myself I would never do: I took cash advances off of my credit card to pay my bills. I thought to myself, *could anything else in my already chaotic life go wrong?* Just as I was asking myself this question, my 2007 Jeep started giving me issues. Thank goodness for an amazing credit score, which I had been able to maintain despite the financial struggles. While at the mechanic, I had to apply for a GoodYear credit card to get my car fixed. This particular credit card had an annual percentage rate (APR) of 27 percent, which is extremely high, but I had no choice. I needed my car.

Soon after being employed as a life insurance agent and seeing that I wasn't progressing in terms of increasing my income, I left. I honestly couldn't take it anymore. I couldn't take working and only being compensated when my policies closed. Needless to say, I was back to square one with no savings and no income. The only thing that I had to hold me was my faith in GOD, as I knew that eventually it would stop raining.

Although I pretended that things were fine on the outside, my life was far from "fine." One Sunday while at church, my mom told me, "You have family to assist you, allow us to assist." My sister within the same week said, "Robin, you have to put your pride aside and let us help you. We know you're a boss and an author, but you can't do this alone. Allow us to help you." These conversations were painful because I *was* those things. I was a published author, I had an accounting degree, and by this time, I had fifteen years in the financial industry. This was not supposed to be happening to me. Although these conversations were extremely hard, I had no choice but to put my pride aside and to allow my family to assist me.

As I continued to look for employment, I started doing contractual work as a bookkeeper. Thank GOD for individuals who knew my abilities to execute various financial tasks.

As I began to wrap up 2015, I thought to myself, 2016 has to be better than the last two-and-a-half years. I'm claiming it!

2016

Here I was in another new year with another new mindset. I was determined to push through to the other side. Still getting nowhere in terms of finding steady income, I had to apply for public assistance: food stamps. At first, I was extremely embarrassed. When I went into the office of social services, I wore a sweatshirt and sweatpants, hoping to "blend in" with the other applicants.

As I began talking and explaining my case, the social worker said, "Ms. Haynes, I totally understand why you are here, please don't feel embarrassed. Life happens to the best of us. It's individuals like yourself who I know will not abuse the system. Remember you're a taxpayer. Use the benefits that you've paid for." I had never thought about it from that point of view, and after having that conversation, I felt relieved and no longer ashamed or embarrassed.

A few weeks after leaving the department of social services, I received a phone call from a very dear friend who advised me that her employer was looking for a business coach. Knowing my entire situation along with my skillset, she knew I was a perfect fit for the job. After the interview, the management team told my friend, "I want her. She would be an asset to the partnership and to both teams." *Wow*, I thought, *things were starting to look up*. I was still nervous, however, because I hadn't been offered the position yet.

A few weeks went by, and I still hadn't heard anything pertaining to the position. Although I didn't hear anything, GOD spoke to my spirit telling me to hold on. Just as GOD was speaking to my spirit, I received a text message stating that I had been offered the position. When I got that text message, I screamed and cried. After three-and-a-half long years, I finally had a full-time job with benefits.

The day before I started my new job, I had to go to divorce court. It was at this point that I realized that another chapter of my life was coming to an end. Although my marriage had ended, I was excited to start to my job and to proceed with my life.

Before the judge made her ruling, she said to me, "Ms. Haynes, you're not asking for child support or alimony. Are you sure?"

My response was simple. "The only thing I want, Your Honor, is to keep my last name since I am a published author."

Although I had twenty dollars in my savings account and twenty cents in my checking account, I knew my son and I would be just fine. I wasn't spiteful; there was no need to be. After the judge made her ruling, I walked out of court, and my ex-husband and I parted ways with no animosity or bitterness. I totally relied on my faith and trust in GOD to continue to see us through these moments.

After receiving my first paycheck with my new employer, I was able to pay my mortgage by myself without outside assistance. I was extremely blessed and grateful to my family for assisting when I was going through my financial difficulties, and now, being able to pay a mortgage that was built on two incomes with one income was huge for me.

Summer 2016

Although I was fully employed, I was not completely out of the woods in terms of my finances. I was barely making ends meet. The state of Maryland discovered that I was now employed, which caused my food stamps to decrease from $194.10 to $16.00. I was a little upset at first, and I wrote a letter to social services pleading to keep my benefits, but my request was denied. Through my frustration, I knew eventually things would turn around.

At this point, my son had graduated from high school and was preparing to go off to college. As a mom, I was afraid to look at his tuition statement because I thought to myself, *how in the world was I going to afford his tuition?* For his freshman year, he received some scholarships from the state and from our church, but that still wasn't enough to cover the tuition, so he was forced to take out a student loan.

As I was preparing my son to go to school, I could barely get toilet paper from the dollar store. I felt as if I had failed as a parent. I wanted him to have everything that he needed to jumpstart his college journey; however, I was not in a financial position to give him that. Although he understood, I felt distraught. Fortunately, my ex-husband was able to help in some areas where I couldn't.

After my son went off to college, I decided to enroll in graduate school to obtain my graduate degree. As I began to close 2016 and prepare for 2017, I continued to thank GOD for sustaining me and my son, along with providing me my employment opportunity. Although still in the midst of overcoming financial challenges, 2017 was going to be better than 2016. I declared it!

THE PHONE CALL

2017

It was now 2017—a new year with a new canvas to start fresh. My son had started his second semester of his freshman year and was getting into the swing of college life. I had my goals for the year written down, and I was ready to execute them.

One morning, as I was driving to the office, my phone rang. It was my colleague whom I had just had a meeting with. I thought to myself, *what could he want, we just met a few days ago?* As we were talking, my colleague told me about an opportunity that was being piloted in Baltimore. Now that I was gainfully employed and enrolled in graduate school, my time was extremely limited. In speaking with my colleague, he informed me that the project was similar to the scope of work that I was currently doing, which was coaching small businesses in Baltimore. I asked what the project entailed, what the time commitment would be, and what the bottom line was regarding compensation.

With a small chuckle in his voice, my colleague said, "Send me over your resume, and I will forward it over to the team."

My colleague told me that I'd be receiving a phone call from one of the executive directors of the program. For the life of me, I still didn't know all of the logistics of the project; I just knew that it was an opportunity for me to make additional income.

A few days went by before I finally received the phone call. The executive director was extremely impressed with my resume. He also mentioned that he had heard a lot of good things about me and that I'd be a perfect fit for the project. I laughed internally and mentally thanked my colleague for making the recommendation to this team on my behalf. When you're good at your craft, allow your work to speak for you. There is no need to brag and boast. Proverbs 18:16 tells us, "A man's gift makes room for him, And brings him before great men" (NKJV).

After going through all of the logistics for the project with the executive director, I was offered the position. I still didn't know the actual role that I'd be facilitating, not to mention I didn't know the team of people I'd be working with, but there were a couple things about this project that caught my attention: I would be making additional income, and I would be assisting established business owners with strengthening their businesses—something that I really enjoyed.

Once I started this project, my free time became nonexistent. Through being a business coach for two programs while earning my graduate degree, I learned the true definition of time management.

After working on this project for a few months, the time had come to be compensated for the work that I had done thus far. The amount that was deposited into my account from the first pay cycle was something that I had never imagined. I was blown away. Just like that, GOD had completely turned things around. I was now in a position to pay all of my monthly expenses *in full*, which was something that I had not been able to do since separating from my ex-husband. The mind-blowing part was GOD had put me in the position of being able to pay my son's college tuition out-of-pocket, by myself. Talk about amazing!

I was finally able to breath financially. And while money isn't always the answer, it did assist with alleviating a lot of stress.

These are the key lessons that I learned during this time:

- Be patient.
- Continue to have an open conversation with GOD.
- It's okay to get frustrated, but don't stay there.
- Even the hero needs a hero.
- The strong, at times, become weak, and that's okay.

THE YEAR OF LIBERATION AND DISCOVERY

"Keep your face to the sunshine, and you can never see
the shadow."
—Helen Keller, Author

2018

It was another new year with another new mindset and a different perspective on life. I thought if 2018 was going to be anything like 2017, I was more than excited. I was *ready*.

As I was continuing to come into my own, my life was in full speed. Although life became extremely hectic at times, I continued to push myself. I made a promise to myself that I would never be in the financial position that I had been in five years prior. Although I kept pushing myself, my work was starting to become affected. I soon learned that I was being "busy" and not "productive." The difference between being busy and productive is simple: we can be busy and not get anything accomplished, whereas when we are being productive, we are successful in accomplishing our goals.

Although my life was moving rapidly, I needed to decompress. I decided to take myself on a trip. I received a referral for a travel agent and made the travel arrangements. Unlike any of my past vacations, I was taking my first trip *alone*. As I began to pack and prep for my much-needed break, I felt electrified. I was excited that I made the decision to finally do something for myself.

That first morning I woke up on the resort in Jamaica, I didn't know what to do with myself. I had no work to do, no clients to see, and no meetings to attend. Simply put, I had no schedule. It was remarkable to sit on the beach and not have a care in the world. I must say that I really enjoyed my time alone. I felt like a *boss*.

As I prepared to return to the states, I knew that once I landed, life as I knew it would resume. It was all good, as I told myself I had to return to the daily grind and prepare to wrap up my graduate degree.

Fall 2018

After weeks of intense work, I submitted my capstone, the final paper for graduate school. Soon after, I found out I had received an A. Receiving an A not only meant that I had passed the final assignment for this particular class, but it also meant that I had finished all required coursework to earn my master's degree in business administration.

When I received my degree, I stood in the middle of my living room floor, astonished. I was now a part of the MBA club, the club that my mom, sister, and brother belonged to. Not only had I received my MBA in entrepreneurship, but I had also been inducted into Delta Mu Delta, an international honor society. Unlike in undergraduate school, where I barely maintained a 2.5 GPA, my graduate school GPA was a 3.82. With the assistance from GOD, along with persistence and determination, receiving my MBA was a major accomplishment for me. This degree was something that I never thought I would be able to achieve.

As I began to close out 2018, I was standing on anticipated tiptoes for 2019. I was ready.

NOW I UNDERSTAND WHY

"Life is about accepting the challenges along the way,
choosing to keep moving forward,
and savoring the journey."
—Roy T. Bennett, Author

2019

A new year with a bigger canvas. So much had happened in 2018. I was truly astonished as to how GOD completely transitioned my situation. I was coming to terms of who GOD was shaping me to be and where HE was taking me. One component that I needed to strengthen was my ability to attend church regularly. I'd always had a solid relationship with GOD—HE was the only reason I didn't lose my sanity during my not-so-good times—but I wanted more. I wanted to fellowship with likeminded individuals who, like me, wanted to strengthen their Christian walk.

Before 2018 ended, I made the difficult decision to leave the church that I grew up in. This church had been my family's church since I was a child, so leaving was extremely tough, but I knew and understood GOD was shifting me into a new season, which meant I had to be in alignment with what HE was preparing me for. After I turned in my resignation to the administrative staff, I joined my current ministry. I knew this place of worship was where GOD needed me to be.

Looking back, I now have a full understanding as to why 2012 to 2017 had to happen. GOD wasn't punishing me; HE was simply preparing me for now.

In 2012, GOD told me to "teach HIS people about financial sustainability." Here I was, seven years later, through the ups and downs, the good and not-so-good times, still educating and instilling in individuals and business owners the financial principles that I firmly stand on. I'm still amazed, humbled, and honored that GOD continues to trust me with this assignment. GOD, through my continued personal and professional elevation, often speaks to my spirit, saying, "You're just getting started, you haven't seen nothing yet." I laugh because I know that GOD is GOD, and if HE says it, it shall come to pass.

FINAL WORDS

THANK YOU for taking the time to read and understand my journey. It is my prayer and my desire that my story has inspired and enlightened you. The purpose of this story is to encourage you and to let you know that where you are currently in your life *is not* your final chapter. There is and will be a "light" at the end of the tunnel—believe me.

If your current situation appears despairing, GOD has equipped you with the tools needed to overcome this and any situation that life presents. The scripture Philippians 4: 12-13 tells us, "I know what it is to be in need, and I know what it is to have plenty. I have learned the secret of being content in any and every situation . . . . I can do all this through him who gives me strength" (NIV).

Life is challenging, as you know, but you also have to know, understand, and remember that if GOD has and is allowing you to go through the situation,

HE alone will bring you through it. Take comfort in knowing that it will work out! Take my word for it.

Your steps are ordered and ordained by GOD. Allow HIM to direct your path and stay out of HIS way. I know it's not easy because we want to do things our way, but know that GOD's ways are not our ways, and HIS thoughts are not our thoughts. Sit still and allow GOD to do what HE does best.

Peace, blessings, and encouragement,
Robin

ABOUT THE AUTHOR

With over twenty years of experience in the financial industry, Robin R. Haynes is a sought-after financial expert who has appeared on a myriad of radio shows and in a number of magazines. With a mission to educate individuals and small businesses on how to become and stay financially sustainable, Robin authored *The Fundamentals of Finances Applied to Everyday Living*. She is passionate about sharing her story to enlighten and empower her audience with the knowledge that they have the ability to overcome financial hardships.

Robin graduated with a bachelor of accounting in 2012 and a master of business in entrepreneurship in 2018. The same year, she was inducted into Delta Mu Delta, an international honor society. Robin currently resides in Baltimore, Maryland. In her spare time, she enjoys reading, vacationing, and spending time with her friends and family.

To learn more, visit www.robinrhaynes.com